Do You Really Want a Bird?

amicus illustrated

Bridget Heos • Illustrated by Katya Longhi

Amicus Illustrated is published by Amicus
P.O. Box 1329, Mankato, MN 56002
www.amicuspublishing.us

Library of Congress Cataloging-in-Publication Data
Heos, Bridget.
 Do you really want a bird? / by Bridget Heos ; illustrated by Katya Longhi.
     pages cm. — (Do you really want– ?)
 Includes bibliographical references.
 Summary: "Several pet birds (and the narrator) teach a young boy
the responsibility—and the joys—of owning a pet bird. Includes "Is this
pet right for me?" quiz"–Provided by publisher.
 ISBN 978-1-60753-205-7 (library binding) — ISBN 978-1-60753-397-9 (ebook)
 1. Cage birds–Juvenile literature. I. Longhi, Katya, illustrator. II. Title.
 SF461.35.H46 2014
 636.6'8–dc23
                            2012035928

Editor: Rebecca Glaser
Designer: The Design Lab

Printed in the United States of America at Corporate Graphics
in North Mankato, Minnesota.

Date 2/2013 PO 1146

10 9 8 7 6 5 4 3 2 1

About the Author

Bridget Heos is the author of more than
40 books for children and teens, including
What to Expect When You're Expecting Larvae
(2011, Lerner). She lives in Kansas City with
husband Justin, sons Johnny, Richie, and
J.J., plus a dog, cat, and Guinea pig.
You can visit her online at
www.authorbridgetheos.com.

About the Illustrator

Katya Longhi was born in southern Italy.
She studied illustration at the Nemo NT
Academy of Digital Arts in Florence. She loves
to create dream worlds with horses, flying
dogs, and princesses in her illustrations.
She currently lives in northern Italy
with her Prince Charming.

So you say you want a bird. You really, really want a bird.
But do you *really* want a bird?

If you have a bird, you'll need a cage.
And the cage will need perches.

Otherwise…

. . . your whole house will be a cage. And everything in it will become a perch.

To make the cage fun, add toys.
No, not that kind. Bird toys!
You'll need to feed him every day.

If you forget…

. . . he'll be hungry. Being in a cage, he can't fend for himself. Poor birdy!

I ordered room service over an hour ago.

Your bird will eat special seeds. Ask at the pet store which kind is best. Fresh fruit or vegetables are also important.

Without proper nutrition…

BIRD STORE

. . . birdie could get sick, just like people! He'll need to visit an avian vet, or bird doctor.

november

1	2	16	17
3	4	18	19
5	6	20	21
7	8	22	23
9	10	24	25
11	12	26	27
13	14	28	29
15		30	

Vet's Lobby

Even a healthy birdie should get yearly checkups. Don't be surprised if the avian vet sees other animals, too. Do be surprised if the bird doctor is actually a bird.

Your bird will need water to drink, and a warm bath a couple times a week.

You'll also need to clean the cage—
and the area around it—every day!
If you don't…

You missed a spot.

. . . it will stink.

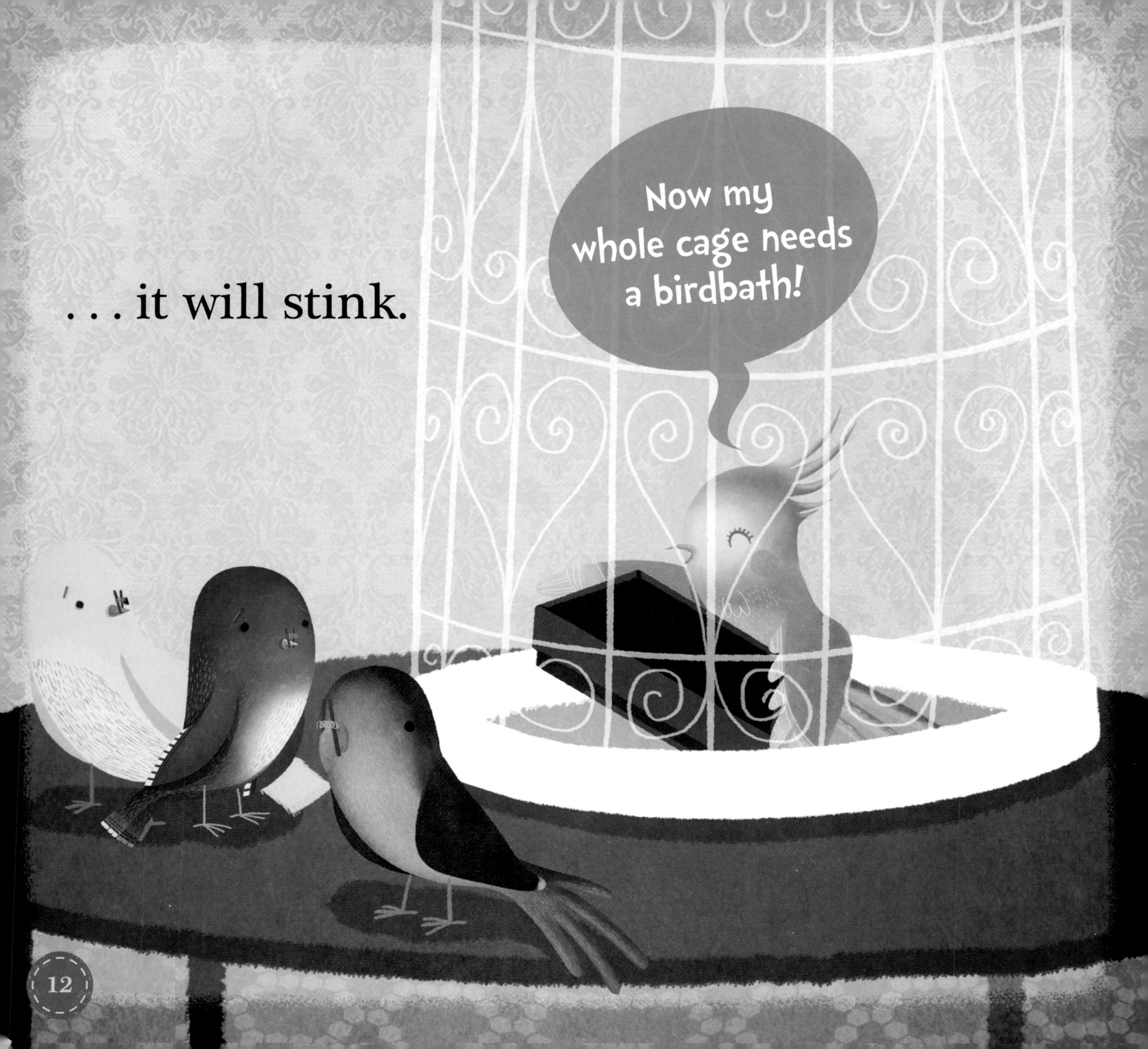

Stinky cage or not, some birds, such as parakeets, cockatiels, and other parrots, don't like to spend all their time in there.

In that case…

. . . you'll need to play with your bird every day.
Hold out your hand. Let him perch on your finger.

Talk to him softly. Teach him to do tricks or say words.

You're smart and handsome!

The two of you can also play
with a toy—like a ping-pong ball!

Unless its wings are clipped, your bird
may fly around the room.

Close the door.

Keep other
pets away.

Hide electrical cords. Close windows.
Pull shades so that your bird doesn't fly into the window.

All cleared for takeoff.

Never let your bird fly freely when you're not watching. **If you do…**

... he could get in trouble.

Some birds, like finches, would rather stay in their cage, with a bird friend. Without another bird, your one bird will be lonely!

I ain't got nobody and nobody cares for me...

Finches and canaries won't want you to hold them.
But you can still talk to them. Birds can be great listeners, too!

I held my friend's new kittens today!

So if you're willing to feed, water,
bathe, play, listen to their (sometimes noisy)
singing, and clean—a lot—then maybe
you really do want a bird.

Now I have a question for the bird.
You say you want a person. You really,
really want a person.
**But do you *really*
want a person?**

Of course you do!

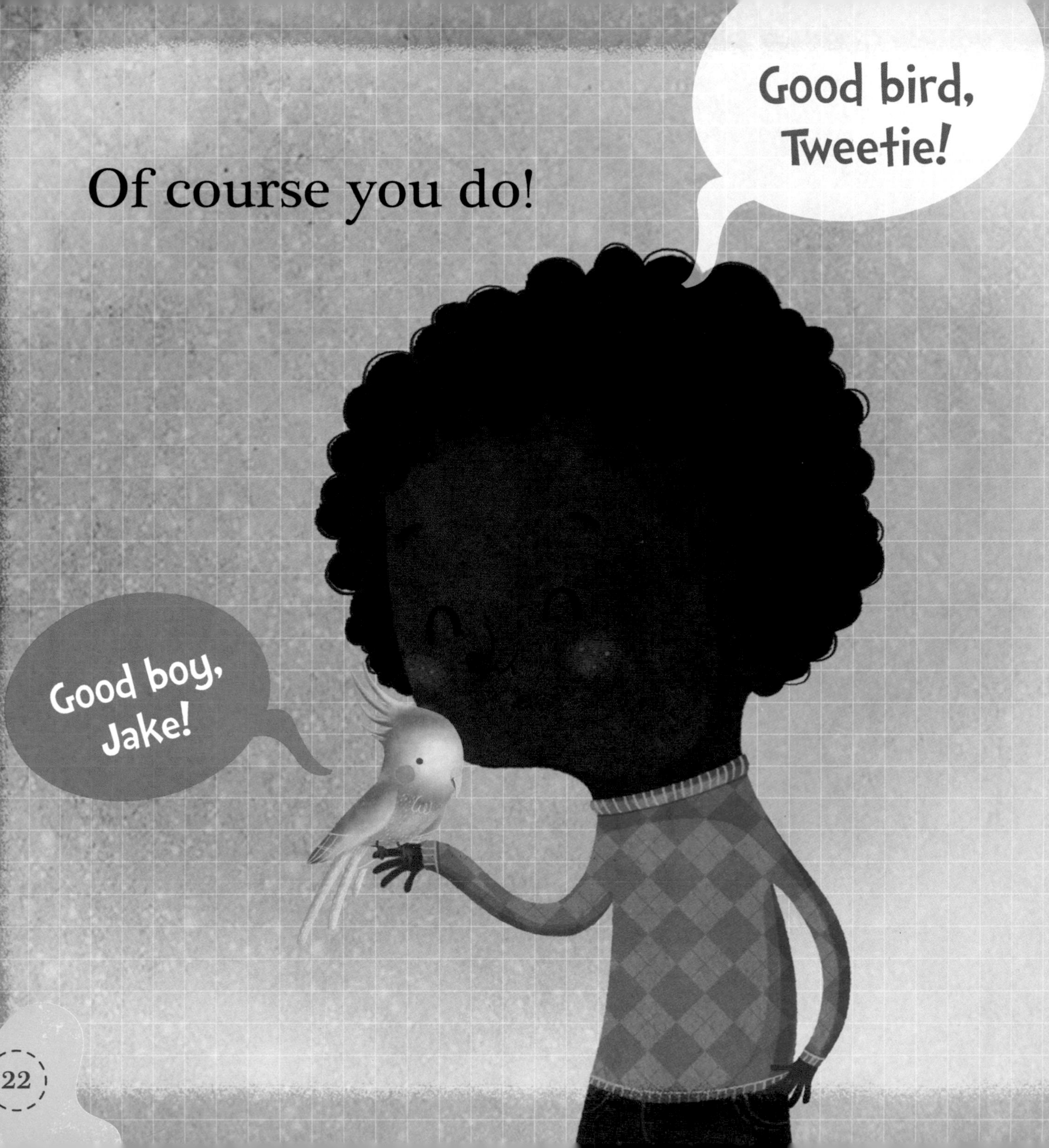

QUIZ

Is this the right pet for me?

Should you get a large or small bird? Could you take care of a parrot? Complete this quiz to find out. (Be sure to talk to breeders, rescue groups, or pet store workers, too!)

1. Do you have a lot of time to train your bird?
2. Do you want to hold your bird and play with it outside of its cage?
3. Does your mom or dad know how to care for birds, and will he or she help you?
4. Do you have room for a large cage?
5. Do you want the bird to stay in its cage?

If you answered . . .

a. YES TO ONE AND TWO, you may want a parakeet, cockatiel, or other small parrot.
b. YES TO THREE AND FOUR, you may be able to raise a larger parrot.
c. NO TO ONE, TWO, THREE, OR FOUR AND YES TO FIVE, you should choose a very small, independent bird, such as a canary or finch. Finches like to live with other birds. Canaries like to live alone.

Websites

ASPCA Kids
http://www.aspca.org/aspcakids.aspx
The American Society for the Prevention of Cruelty
to Animals provides games, photos, and videos that
demonstrate pet care, plus information on careers working
with animals.

Pet Bird Care and Behavior Tips:
The Humane Society of the United States
http://www.humanesociety.org/animals/pet_birds/tips/pet_bird_tips.html
The Humane Society has advice on bird care, cage set-up,
feeding, and choosing the right bird for you.

Parrot Parrot
www.parrotparrot.com
This site offers species guides for parrots, canaries,
cockatiels, finches, and several more, plus bird videos,
photographs, and health information.

Tama and Friends visit Petfinder.com
http://www.petfinder.com/tama//index.html
The kids' section of Petfinder.com offers games, pet tips, pet
listings, and a section for parents.

Read More

Bodden, Valerie. *Birds.* My First Look At. Creative Education, 2009.

Glover, David and Penny. *Owning a Pet Bird.* Owning a Pet. Sea-to-Sea Publications, 2008.

Mead, Wendy S. *Top 10 Birds for Kids.* Enslow Elementary, 2009.

Morgan, Sally. *Birds.* Pets Plus. Smart Apple Media, 2013.

Tweet!